This Coloring Book Belongs to:

_____

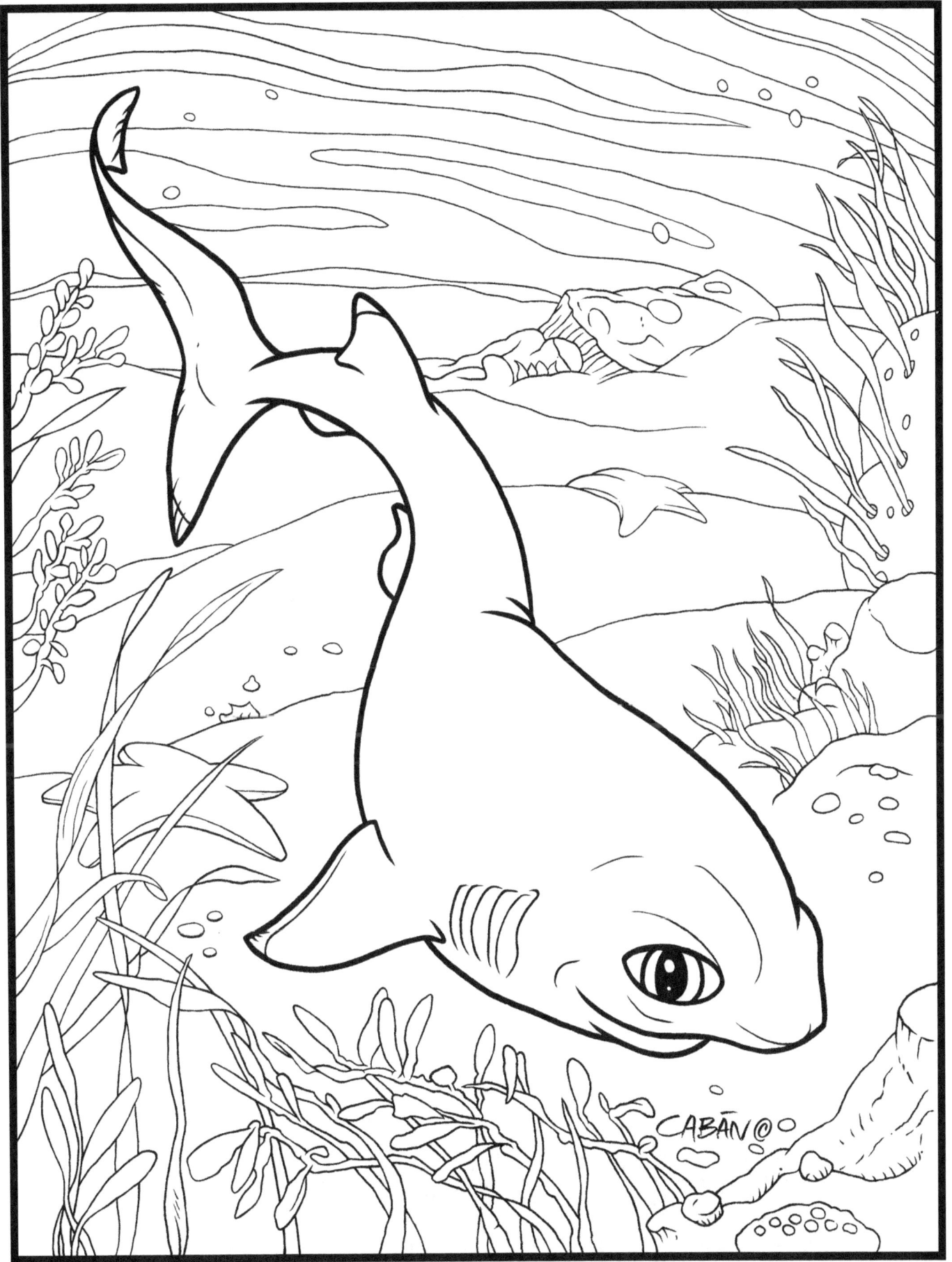

Bigeyed Sixgill Shark

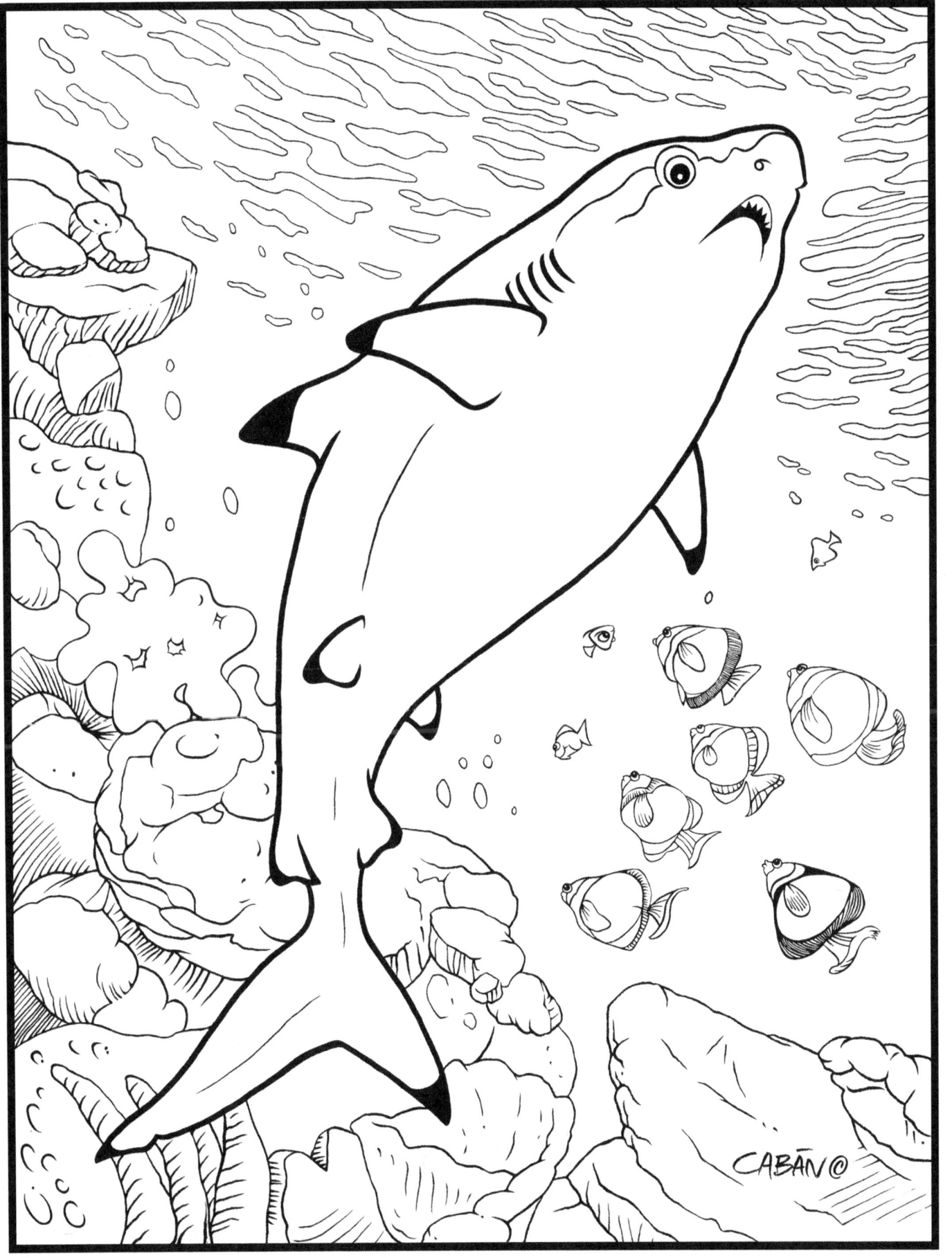

Blacktip Reef Shark

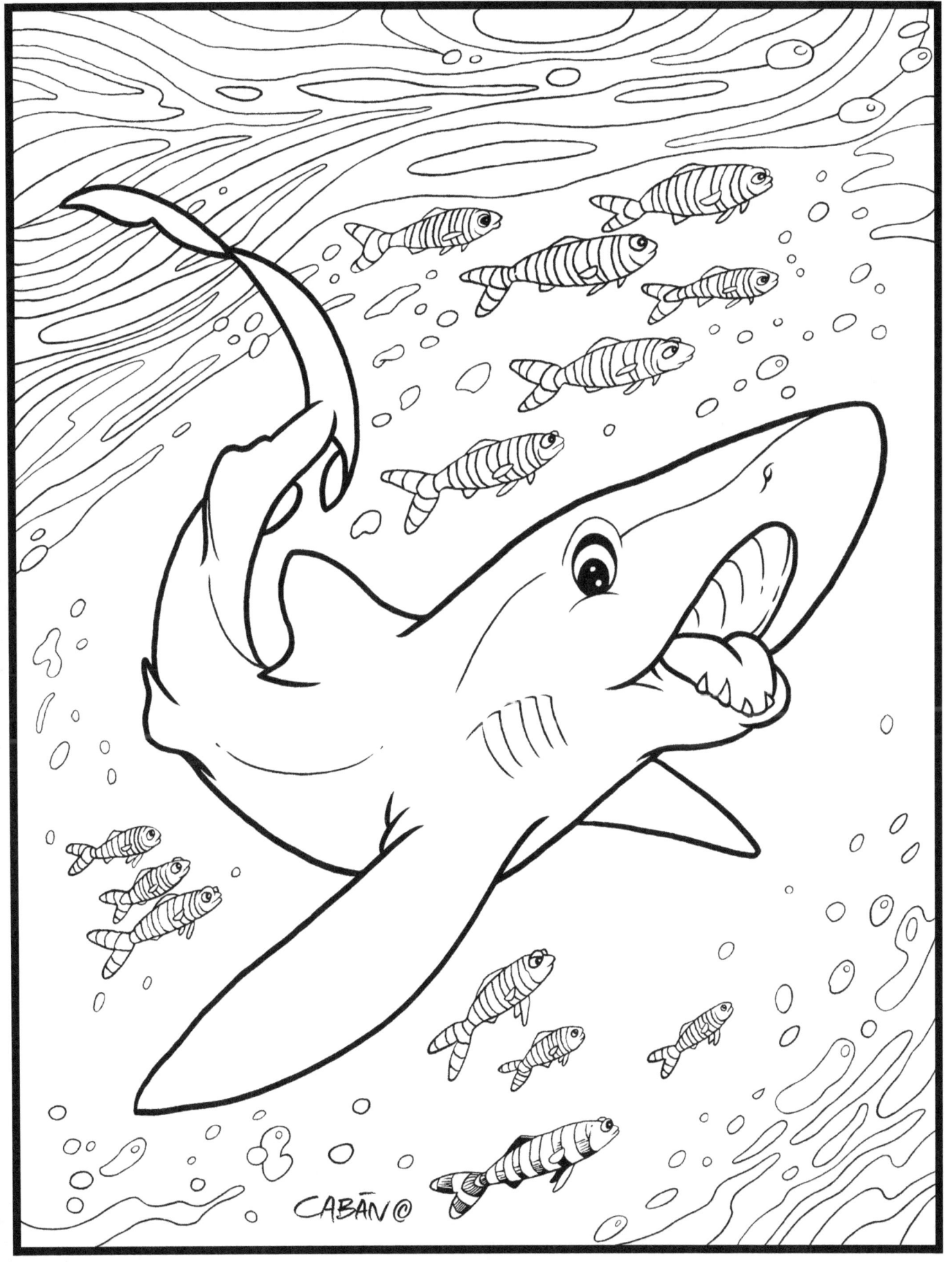

Blue Shark

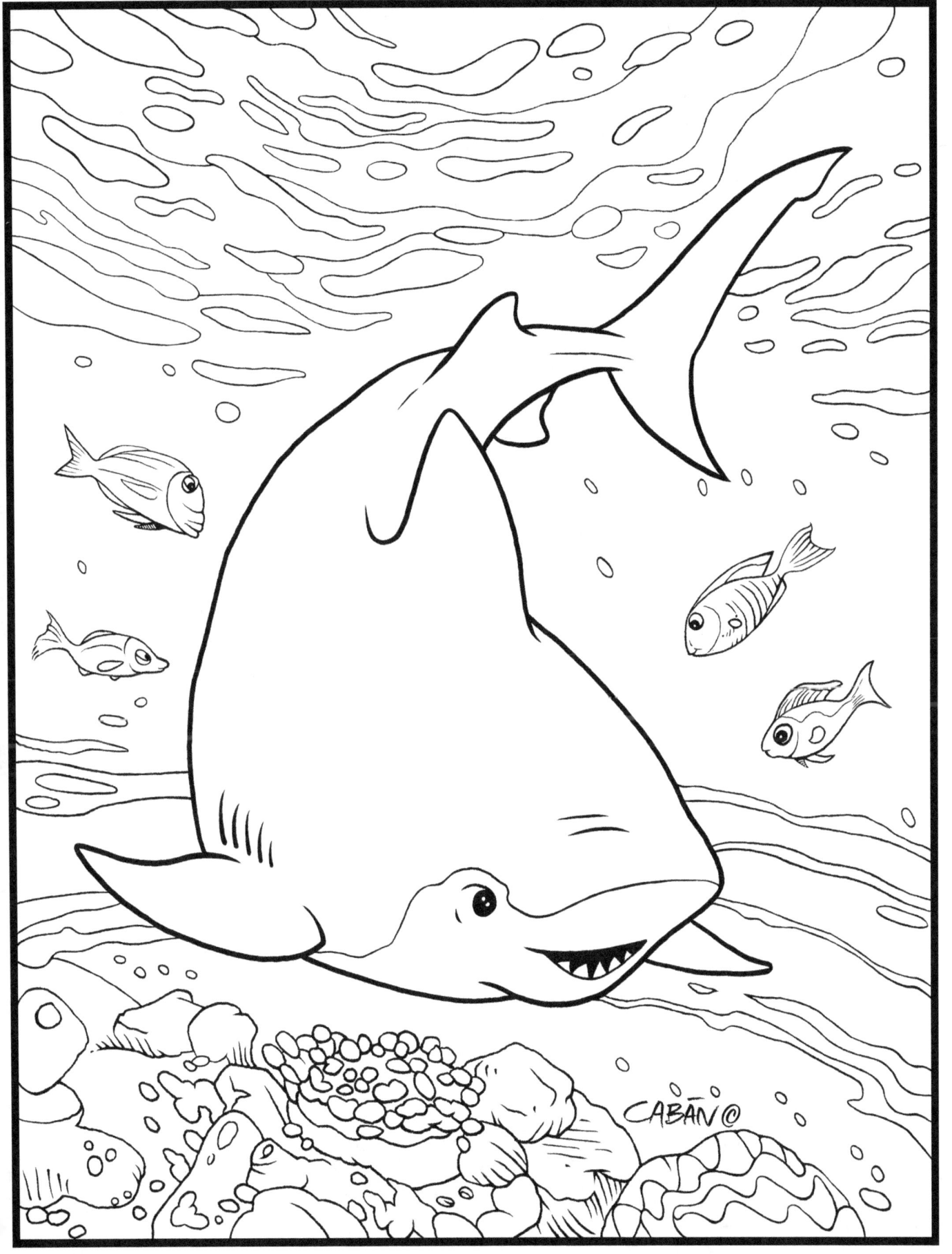

Bull Shark

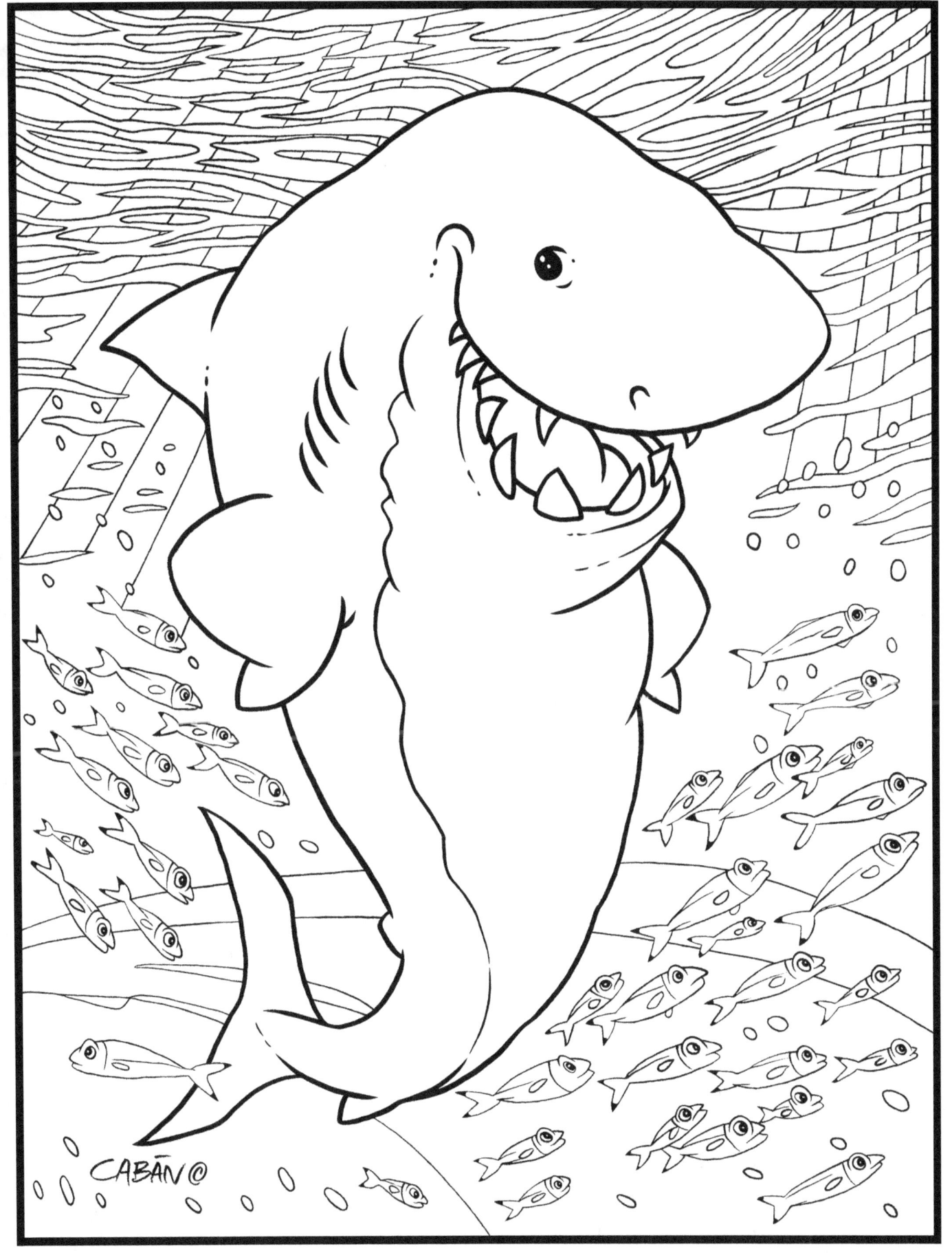

Great White Shark

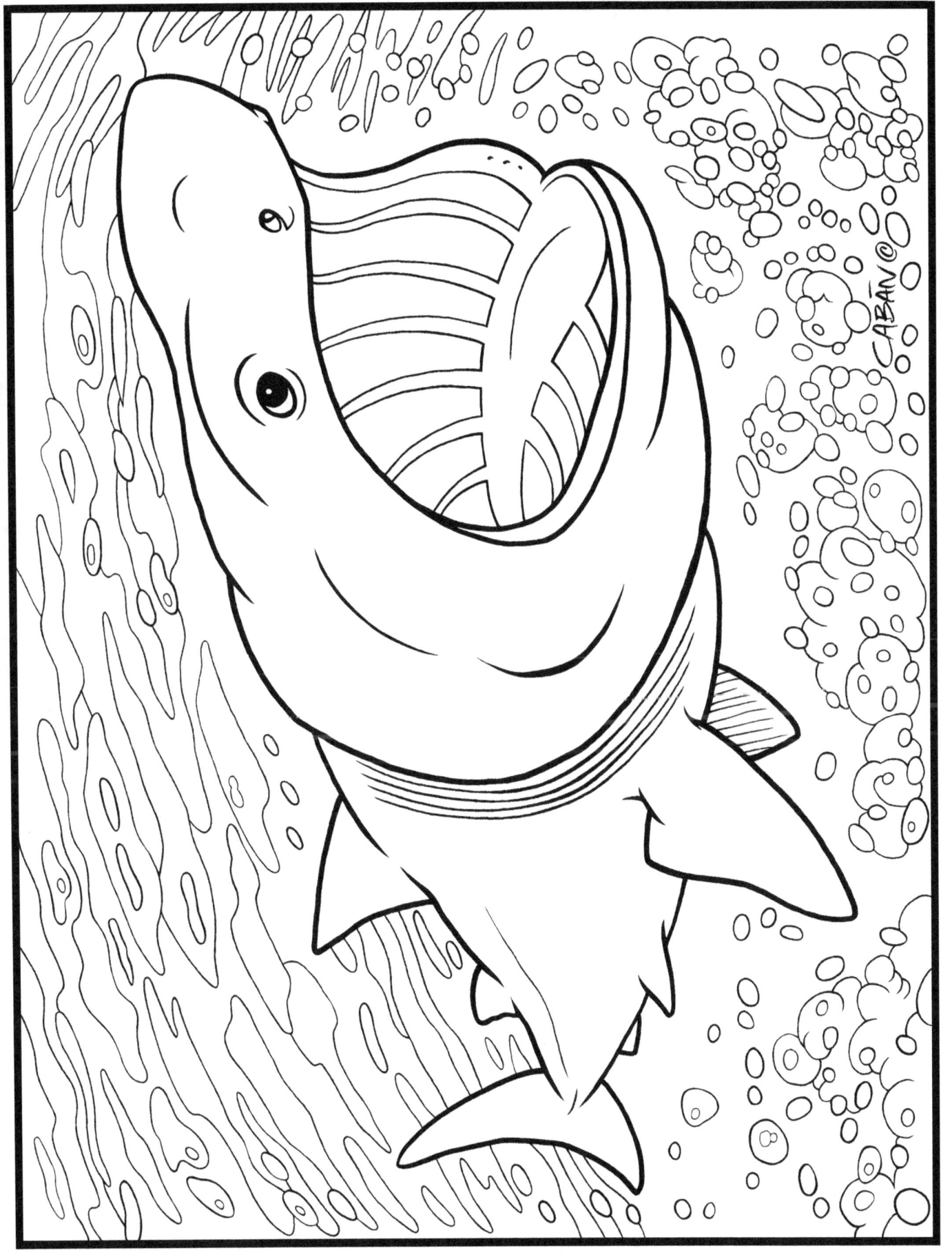

Baskin Shark

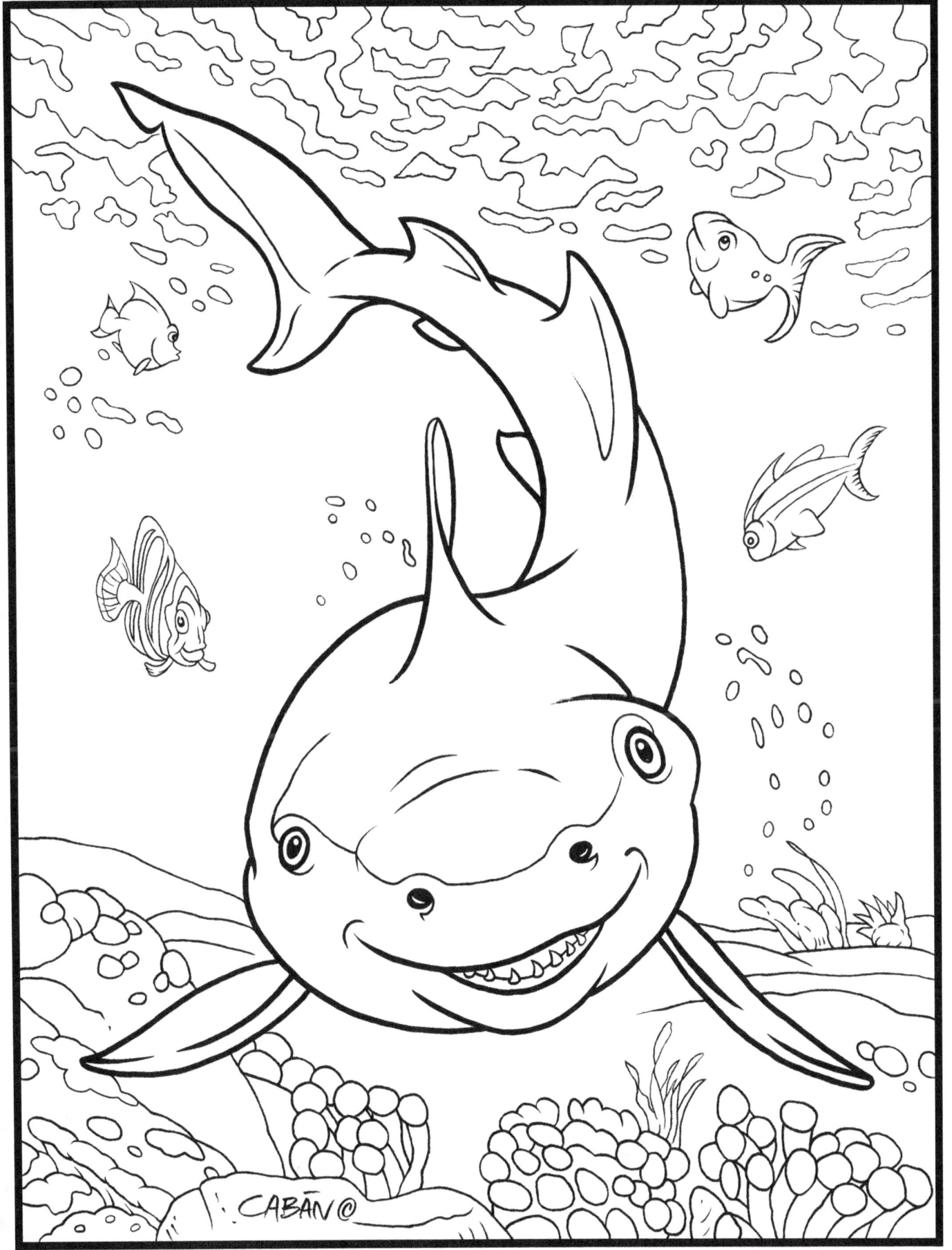

Lemon Shark

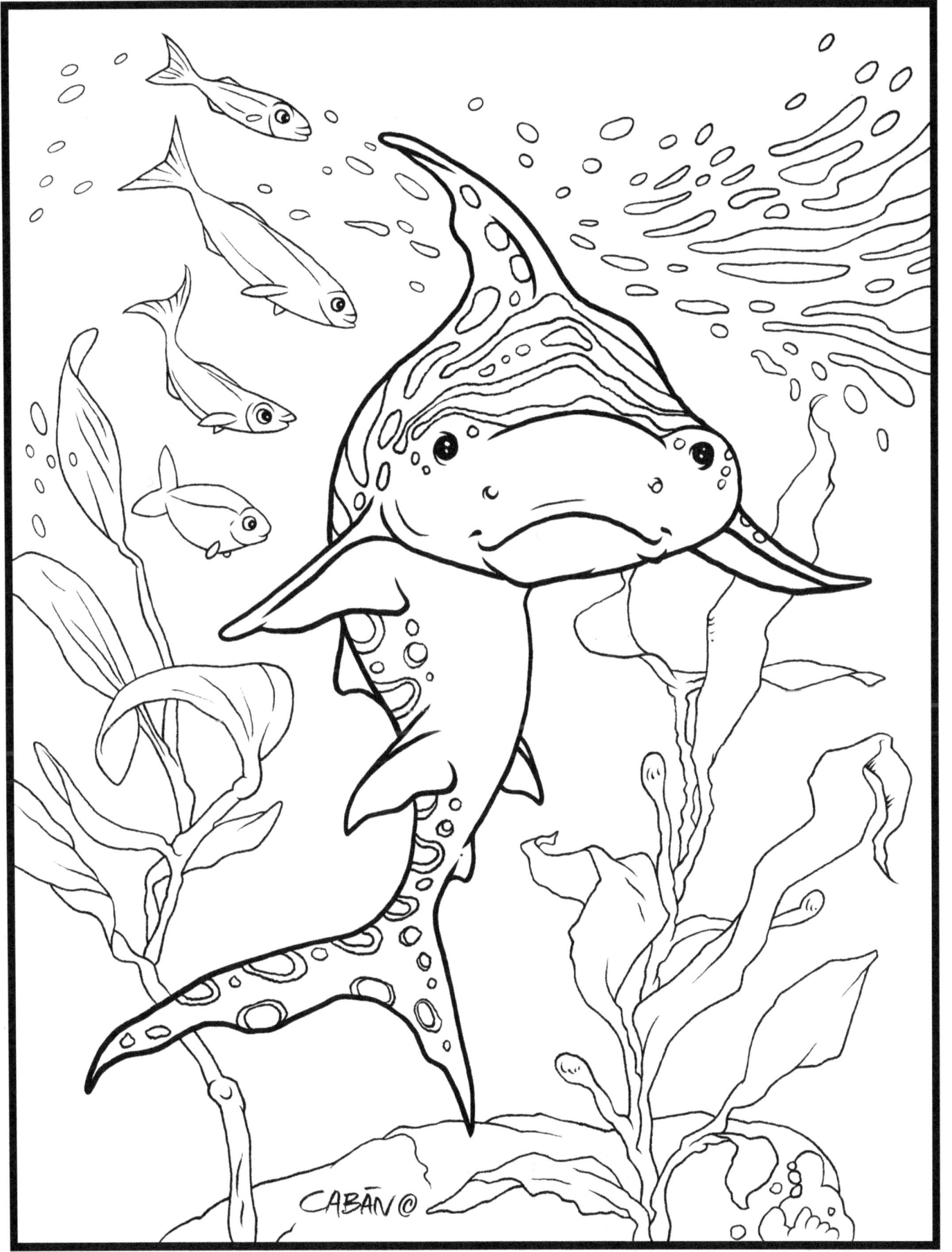

Leopard Shark

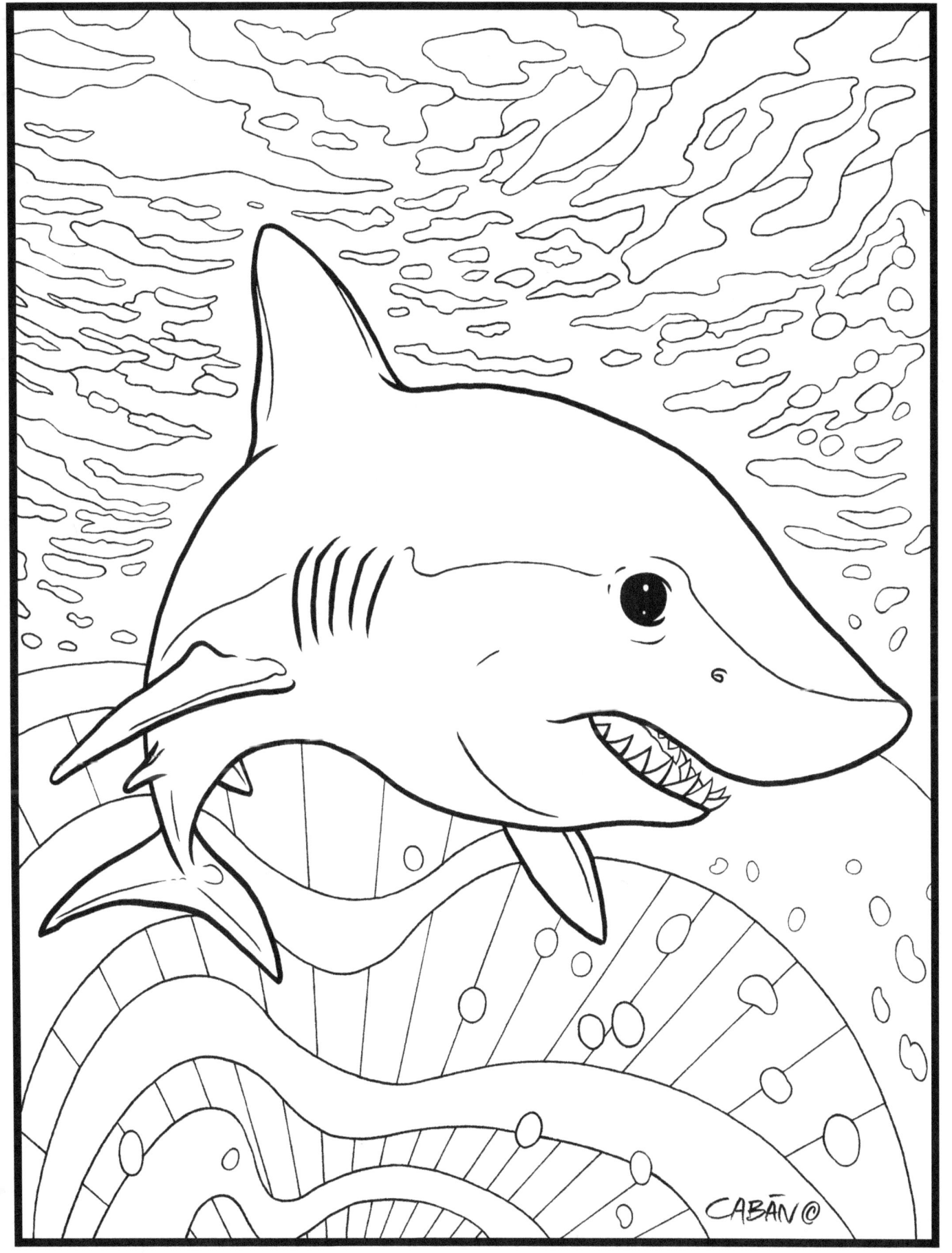

Mako Shark

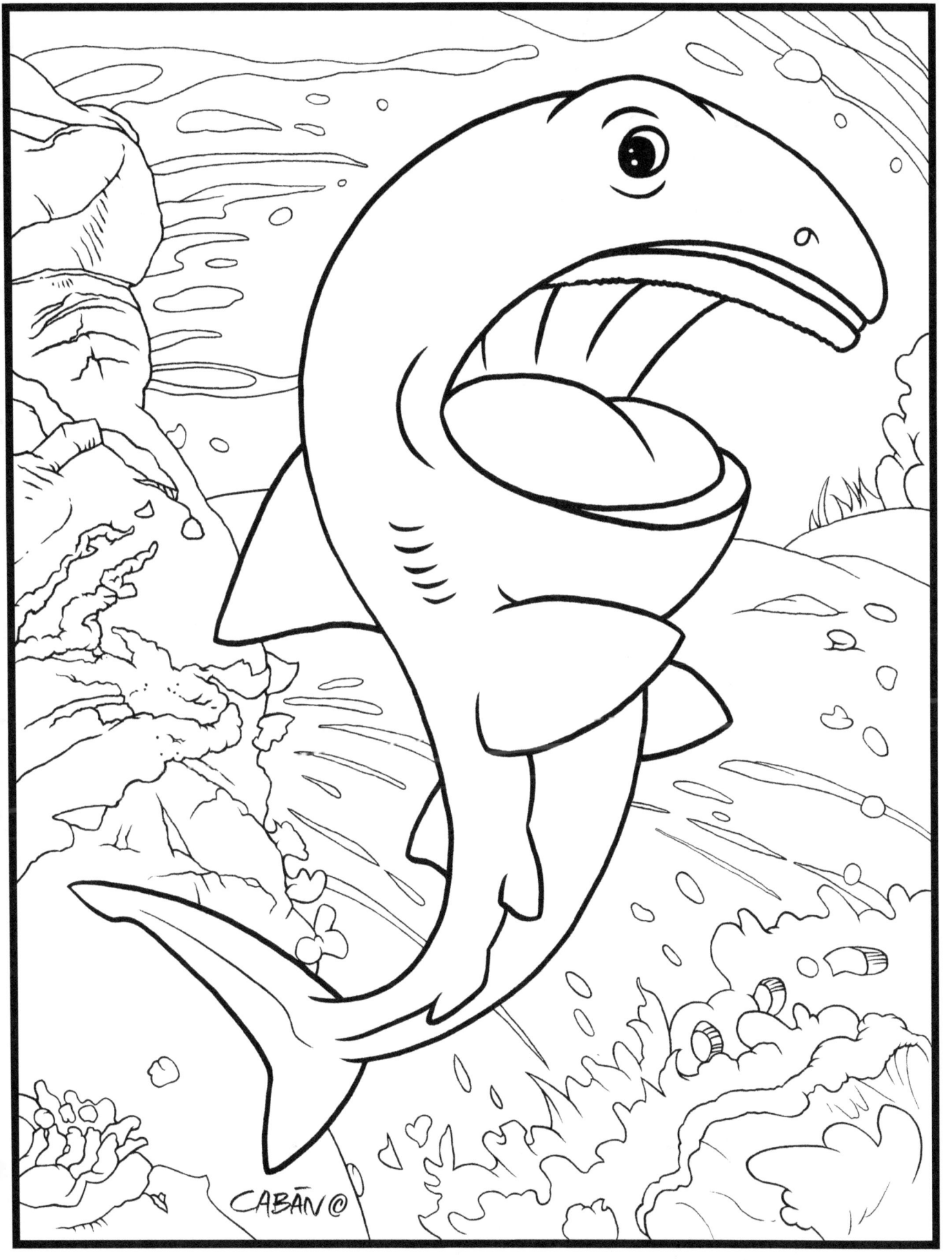

Megamouth Shark

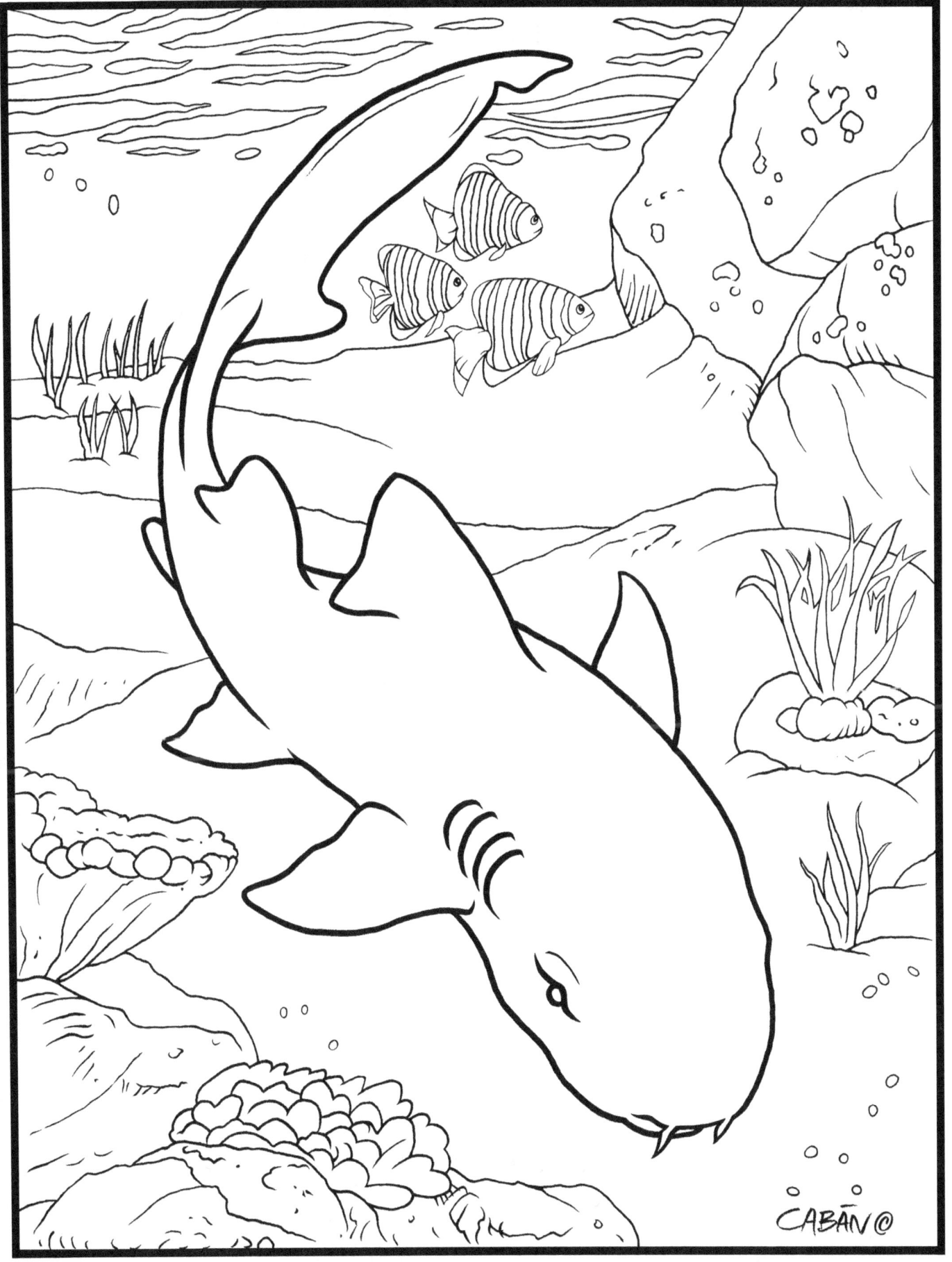

Nurse Shark

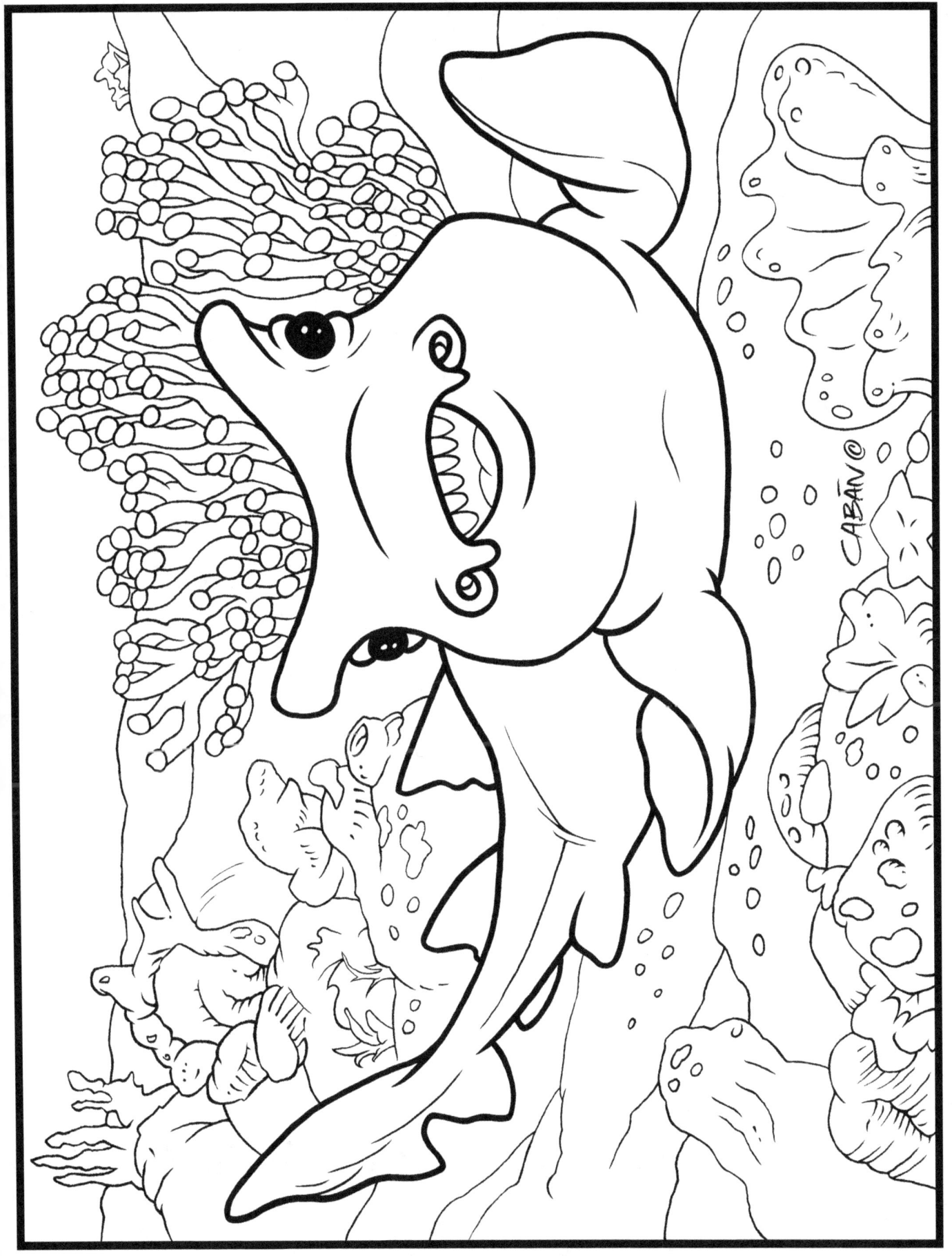

Crested Bullhead Shark

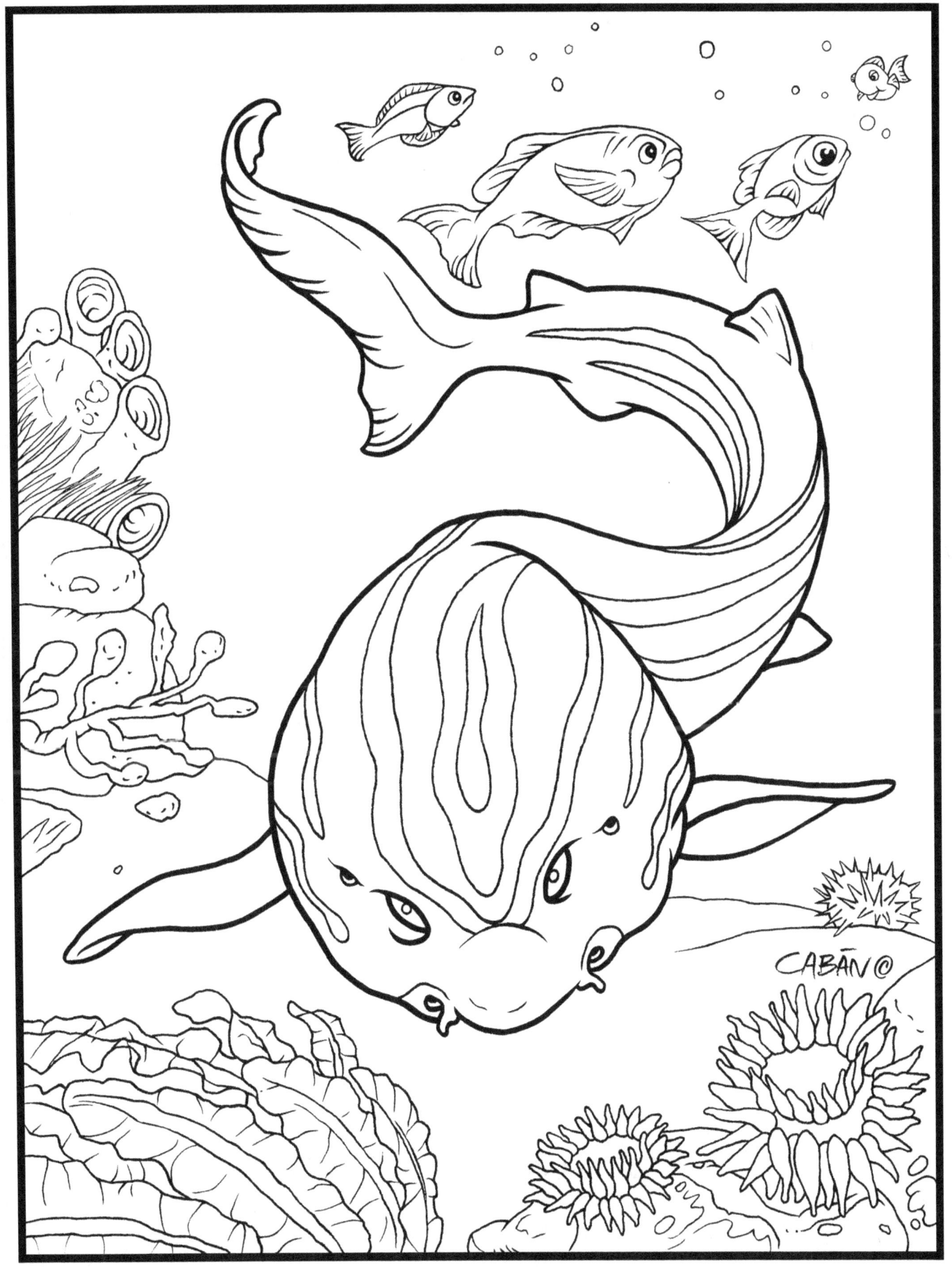

Pyjama Shark

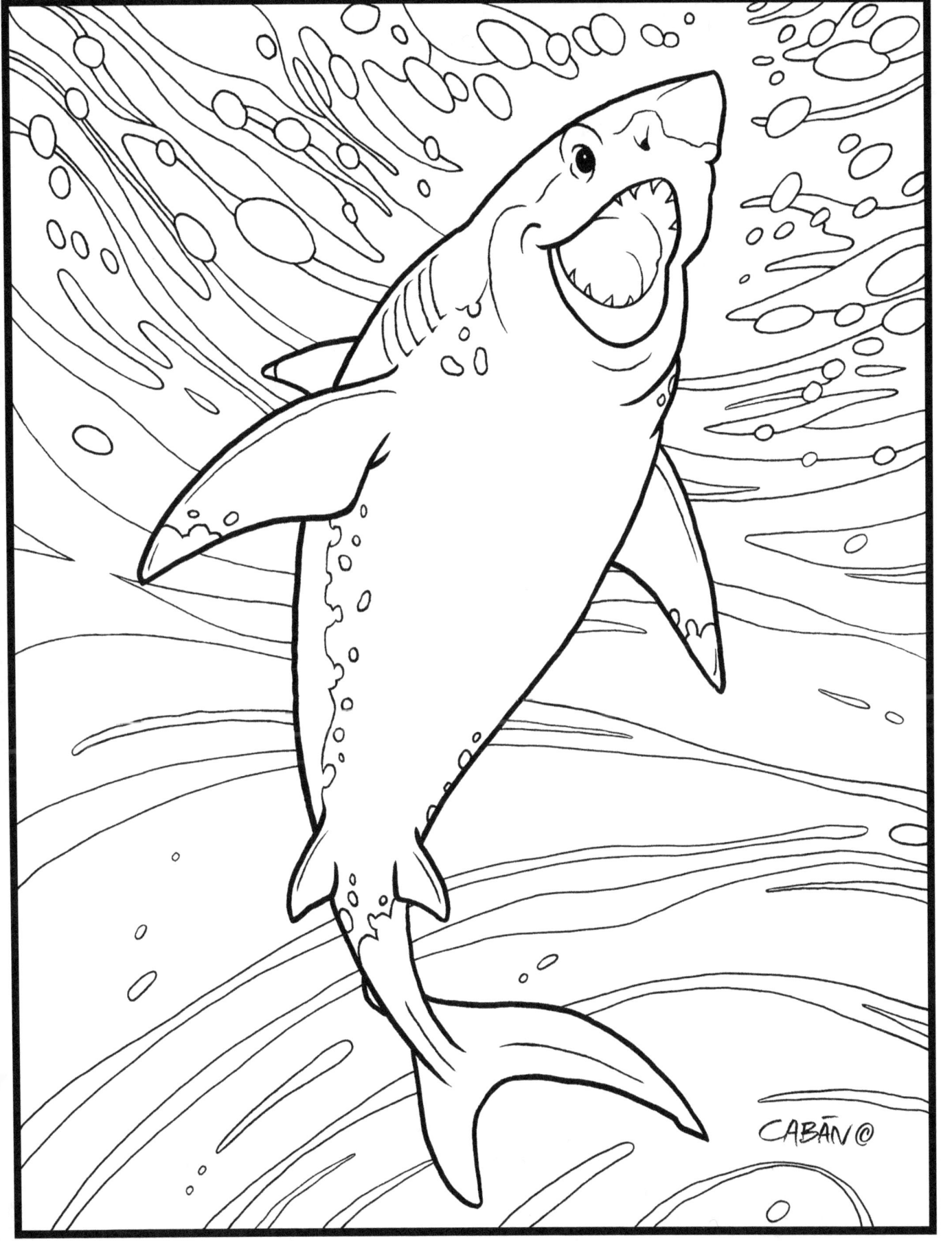

Salmon Shark

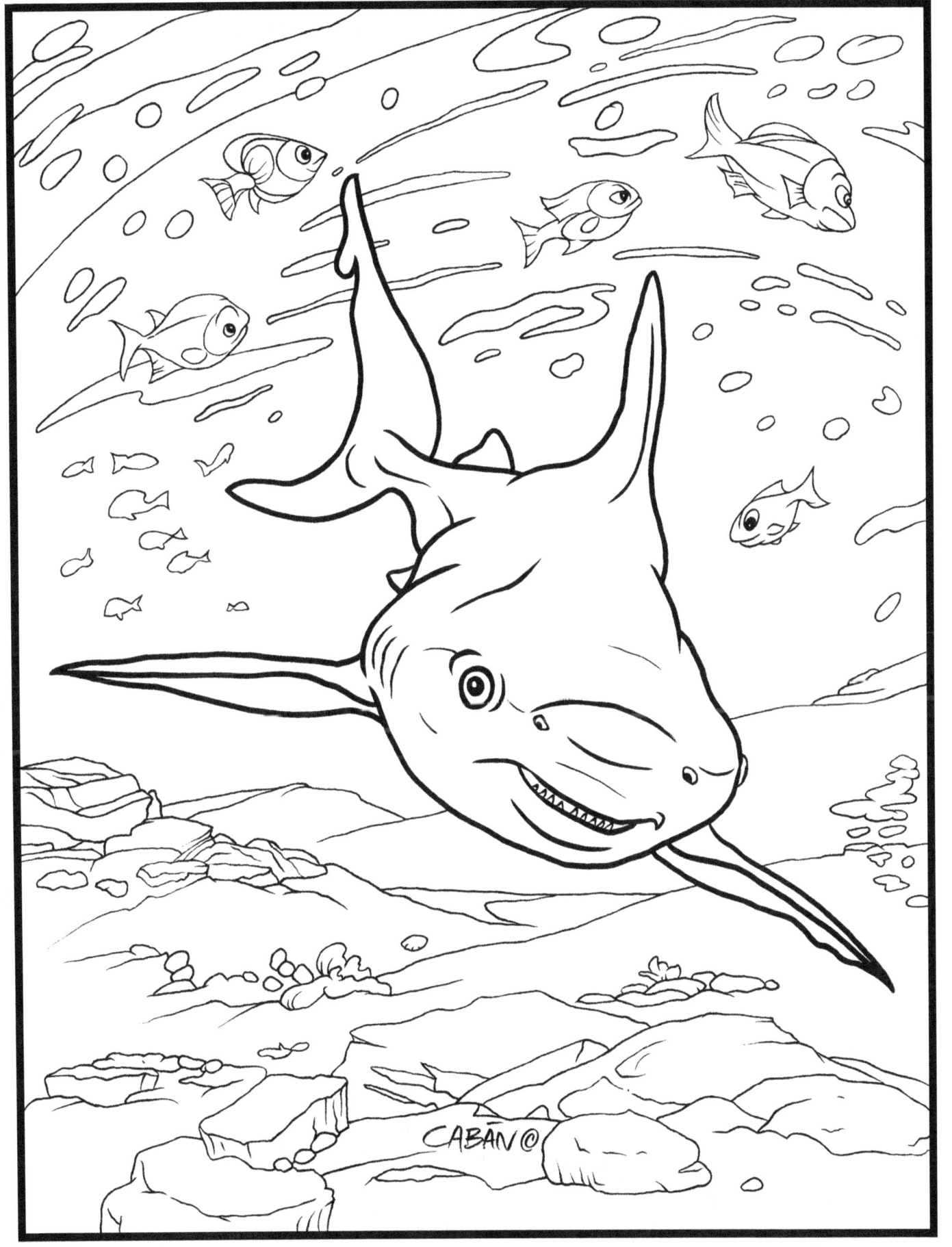

Sandbar Shark

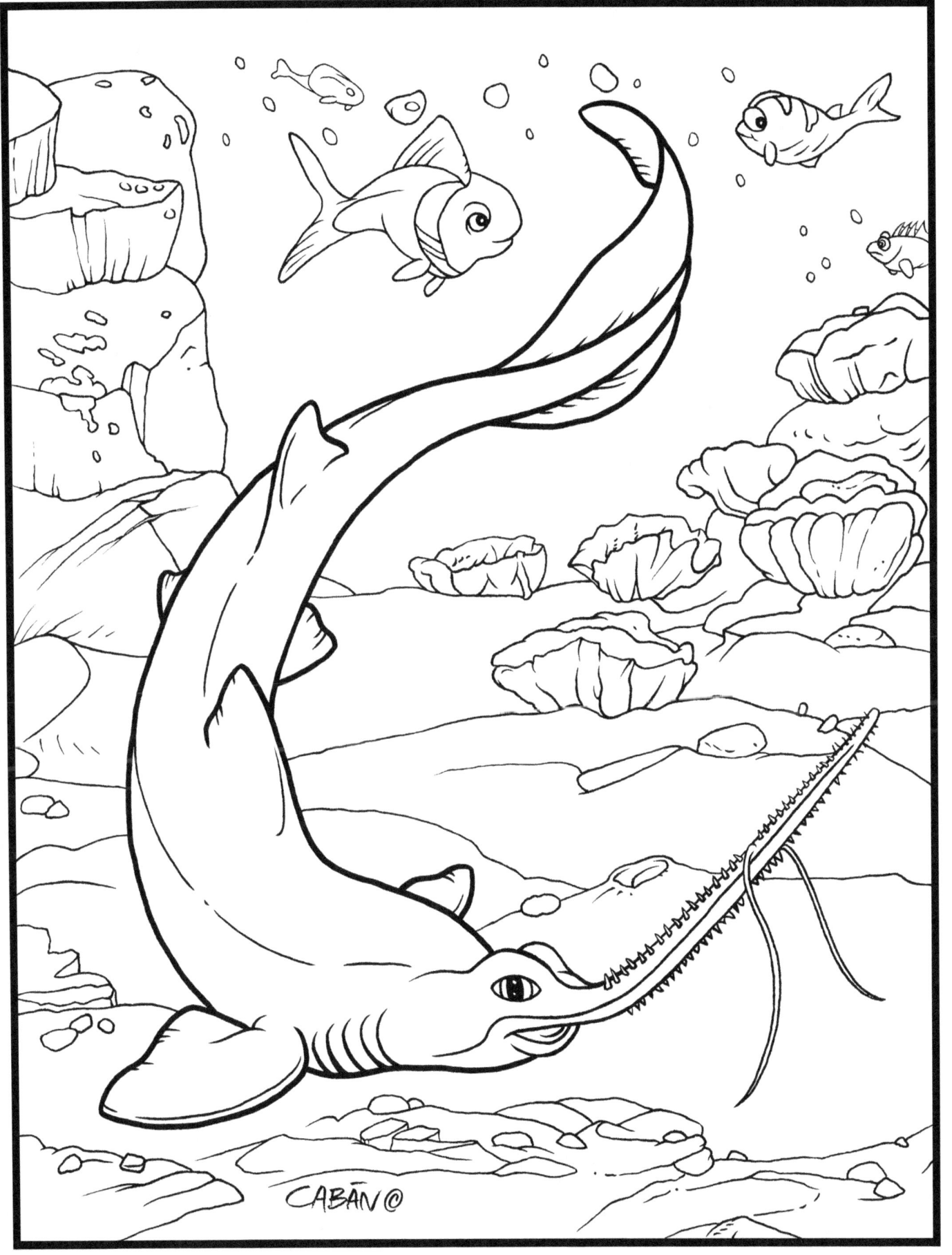

Saw Shark

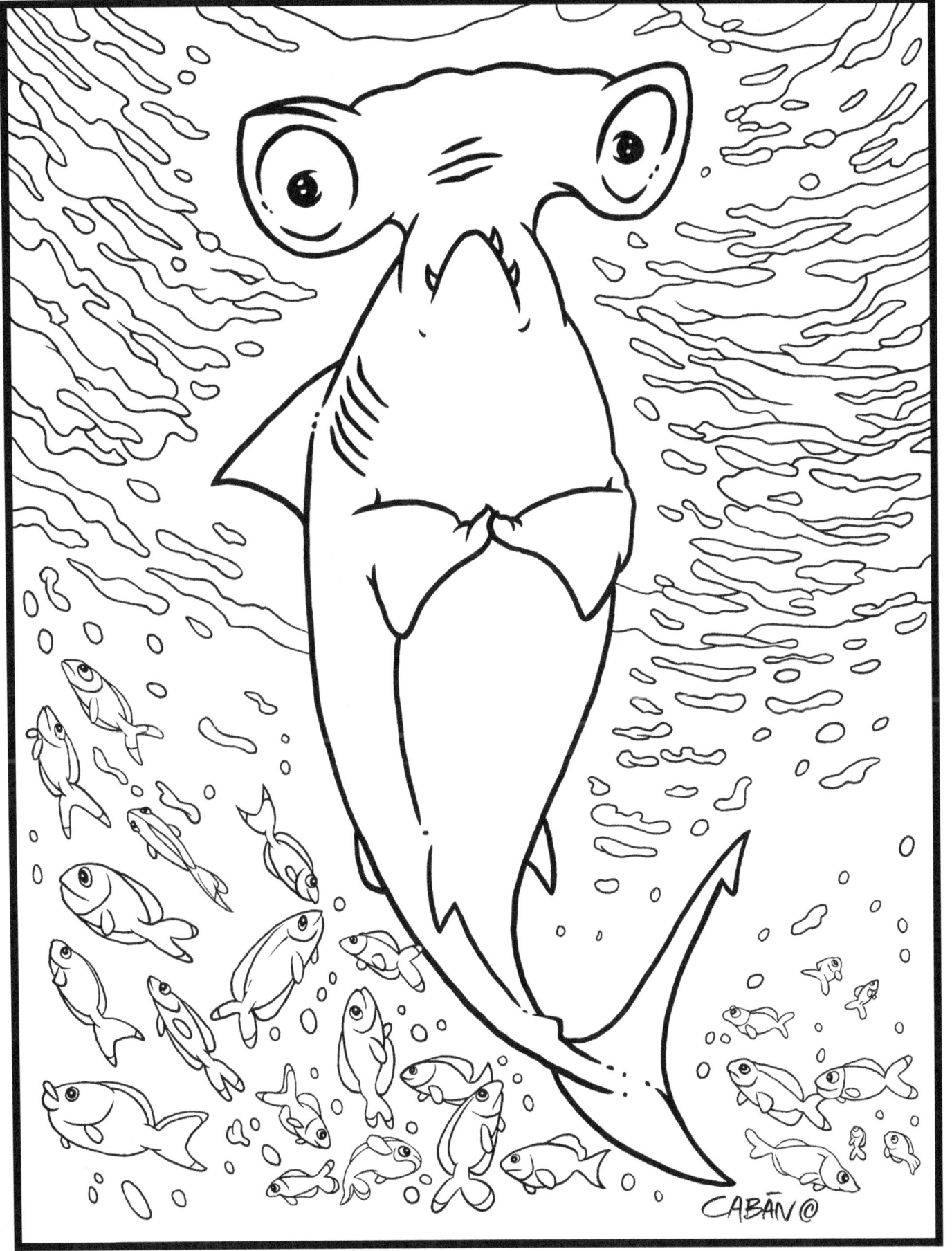

Scalloped Hammerhead Shark

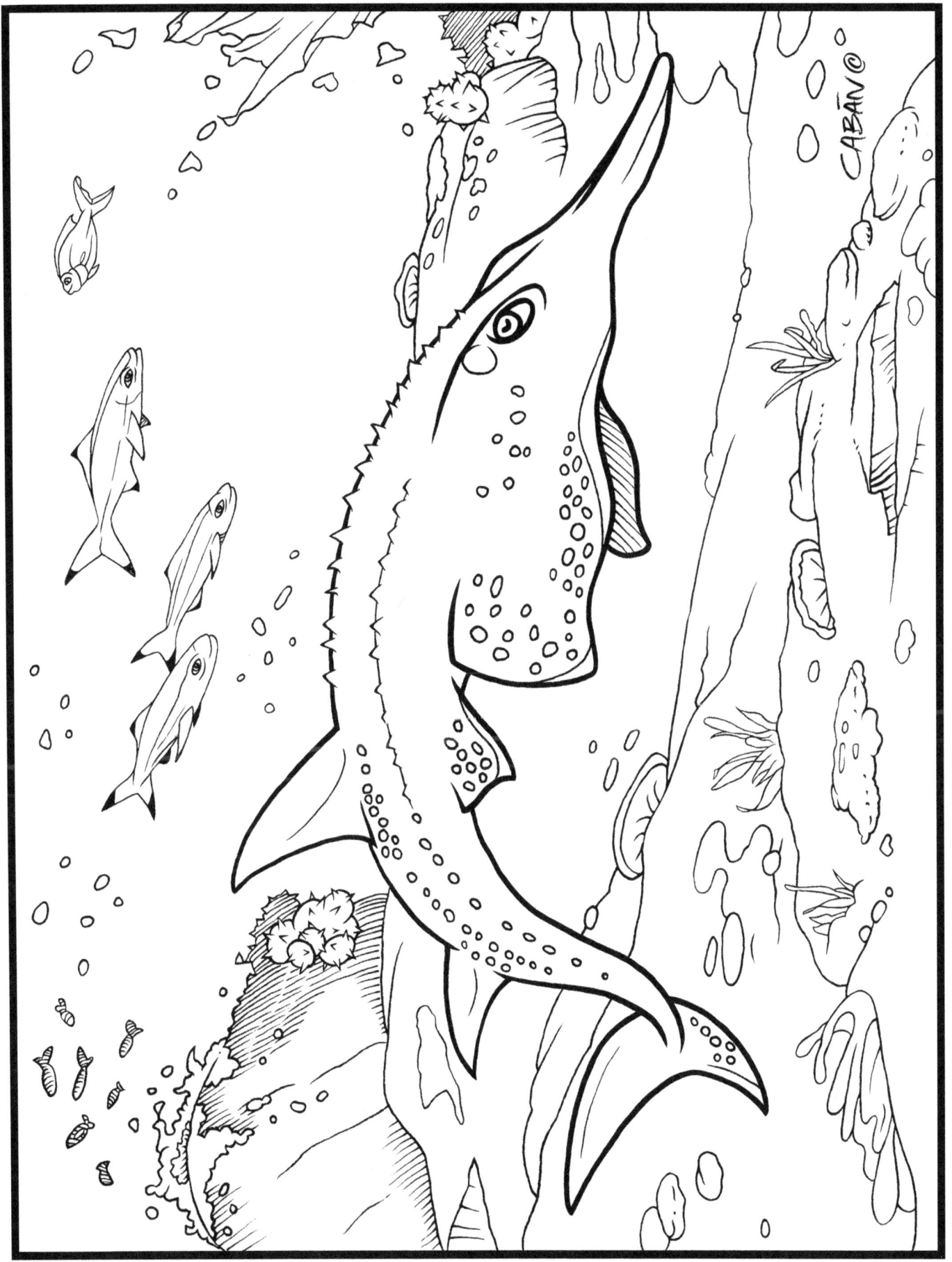

Guitar Shark

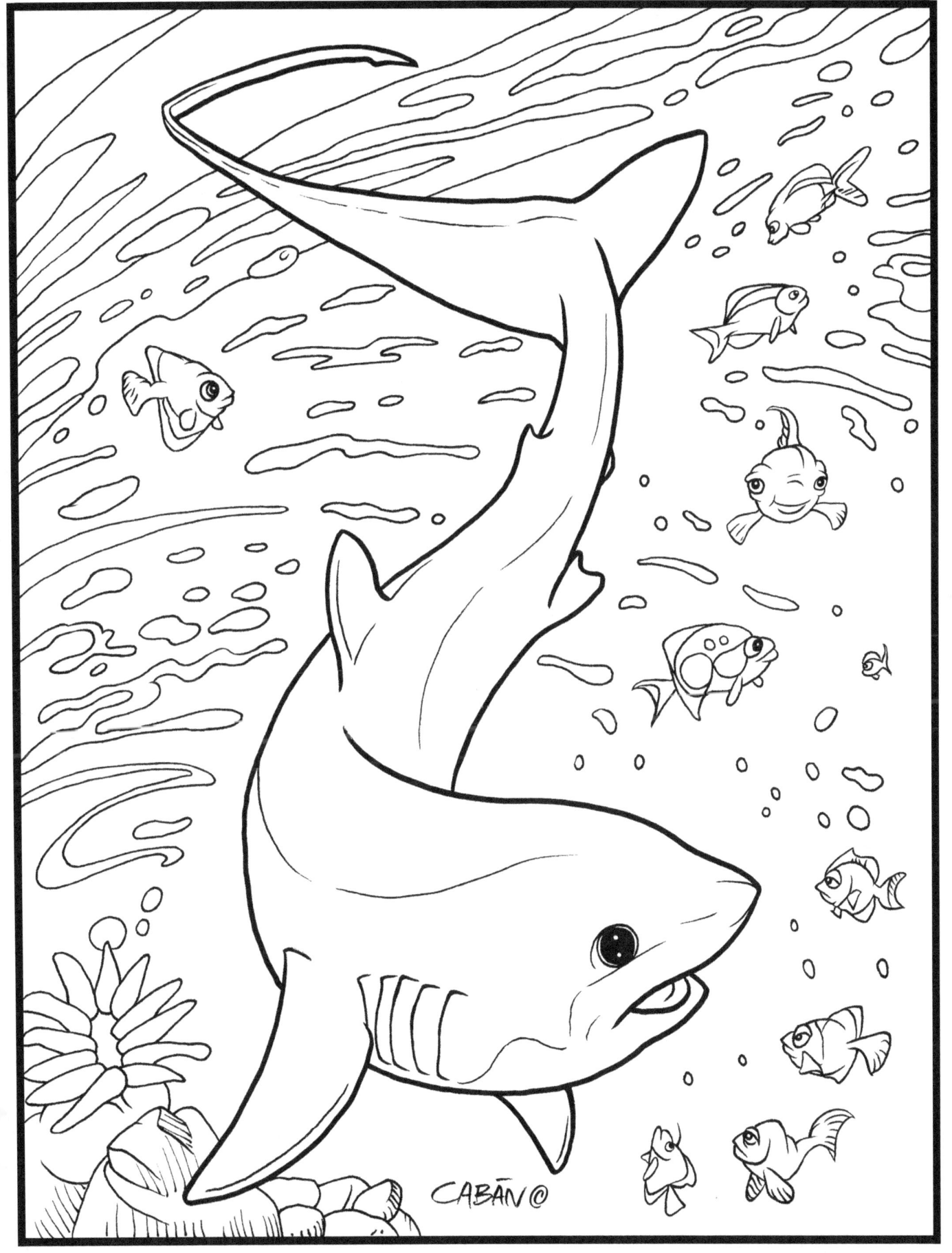

Thresher Shark

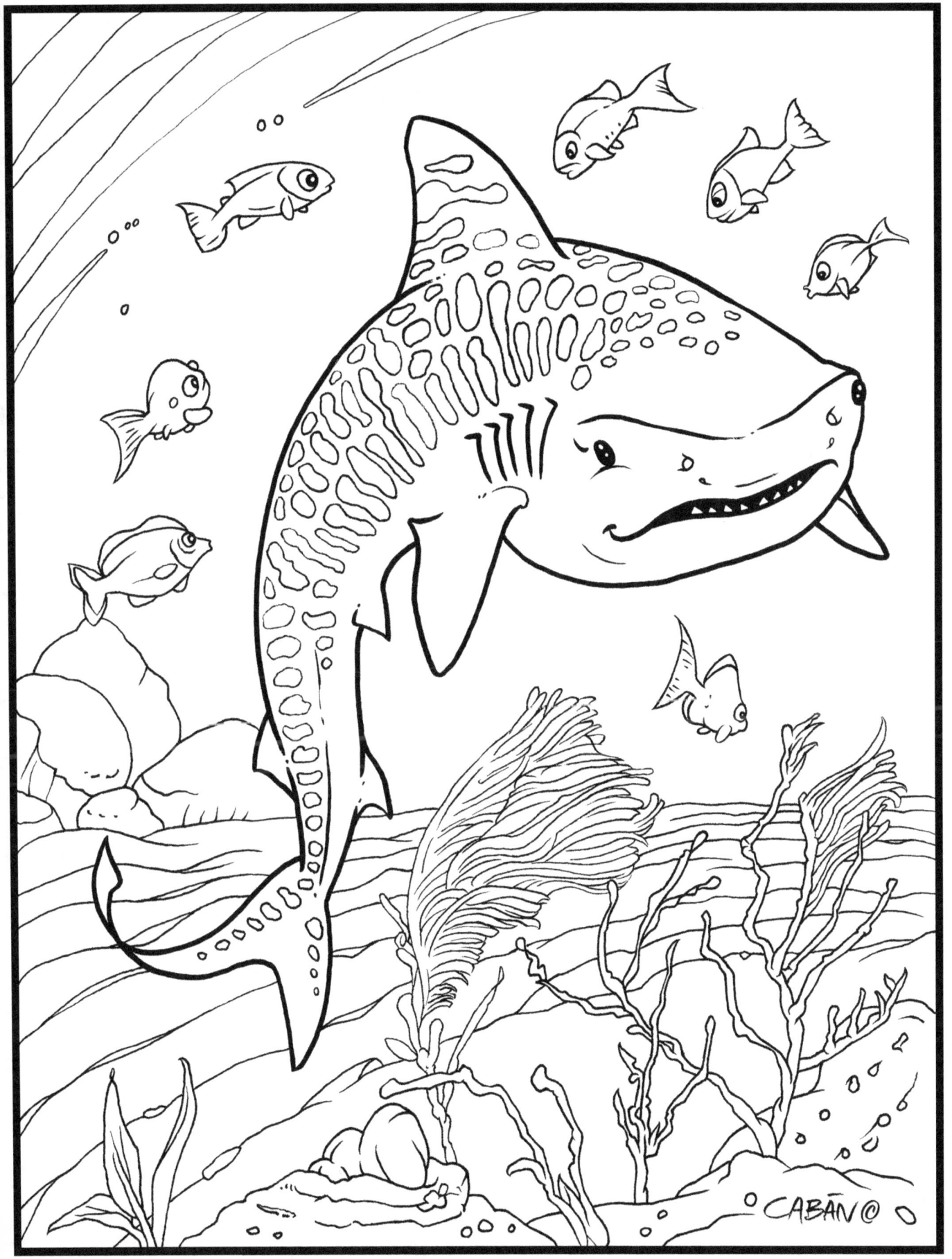

Tiger Shark

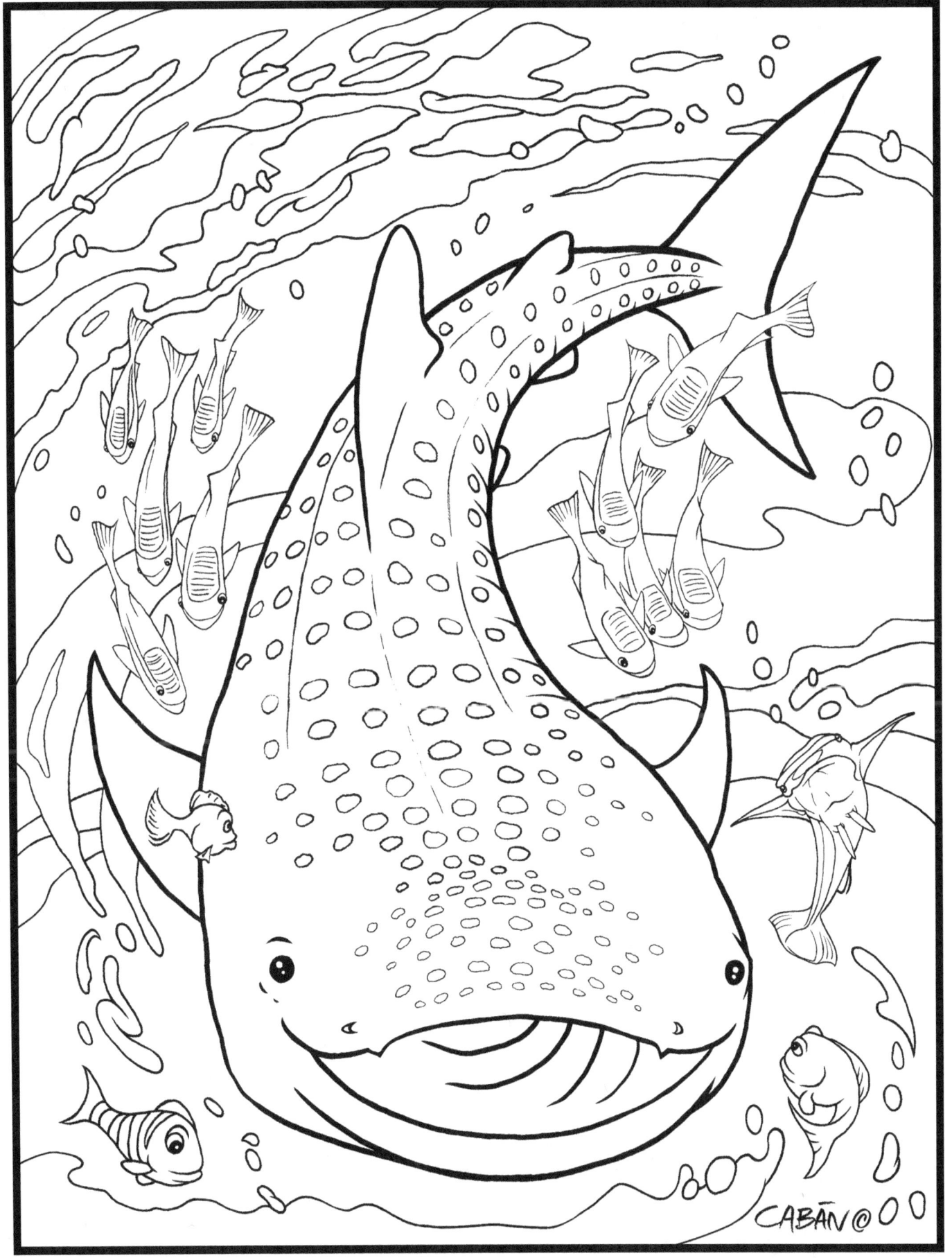

Whale Shark

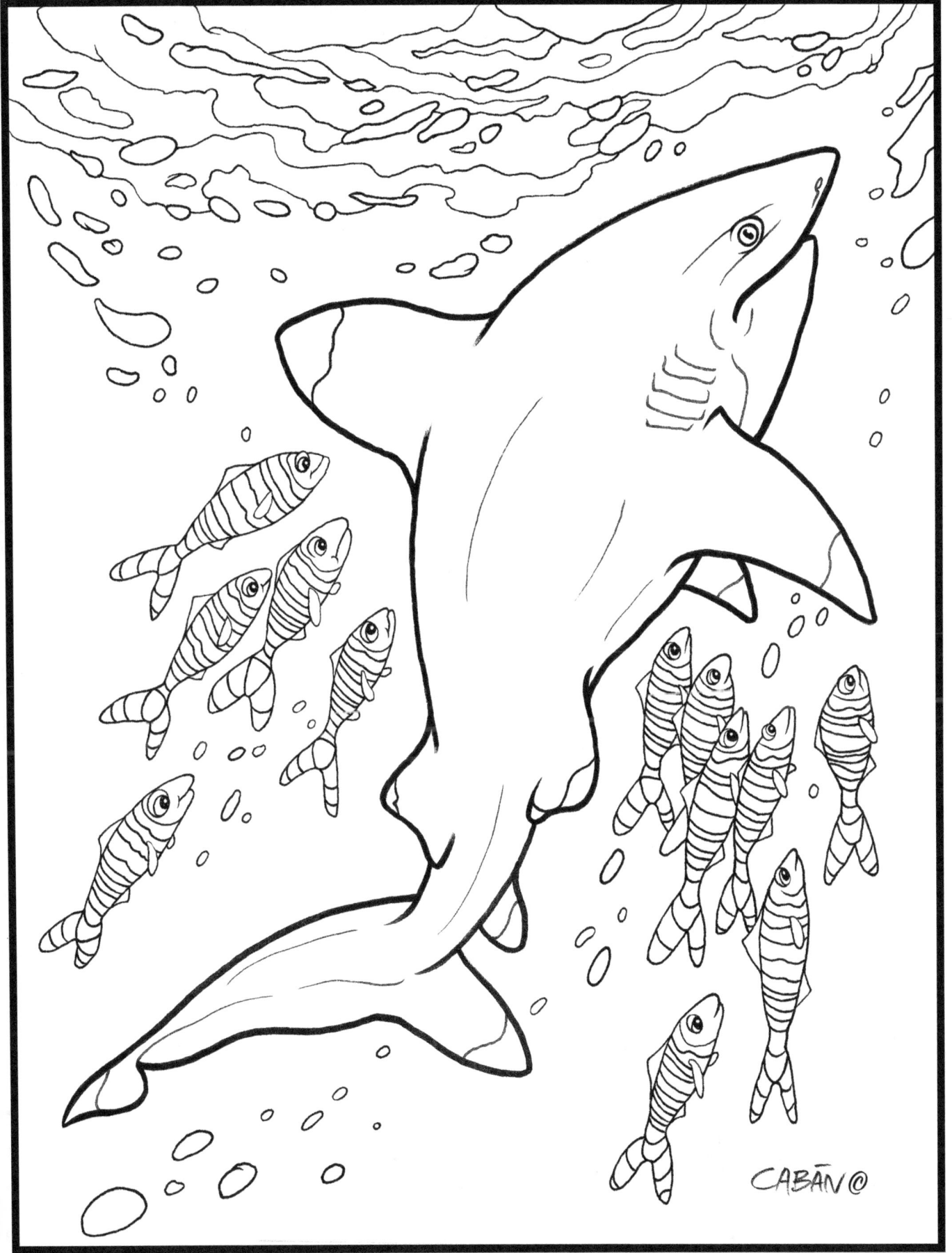

Whitetip Ocean Shark

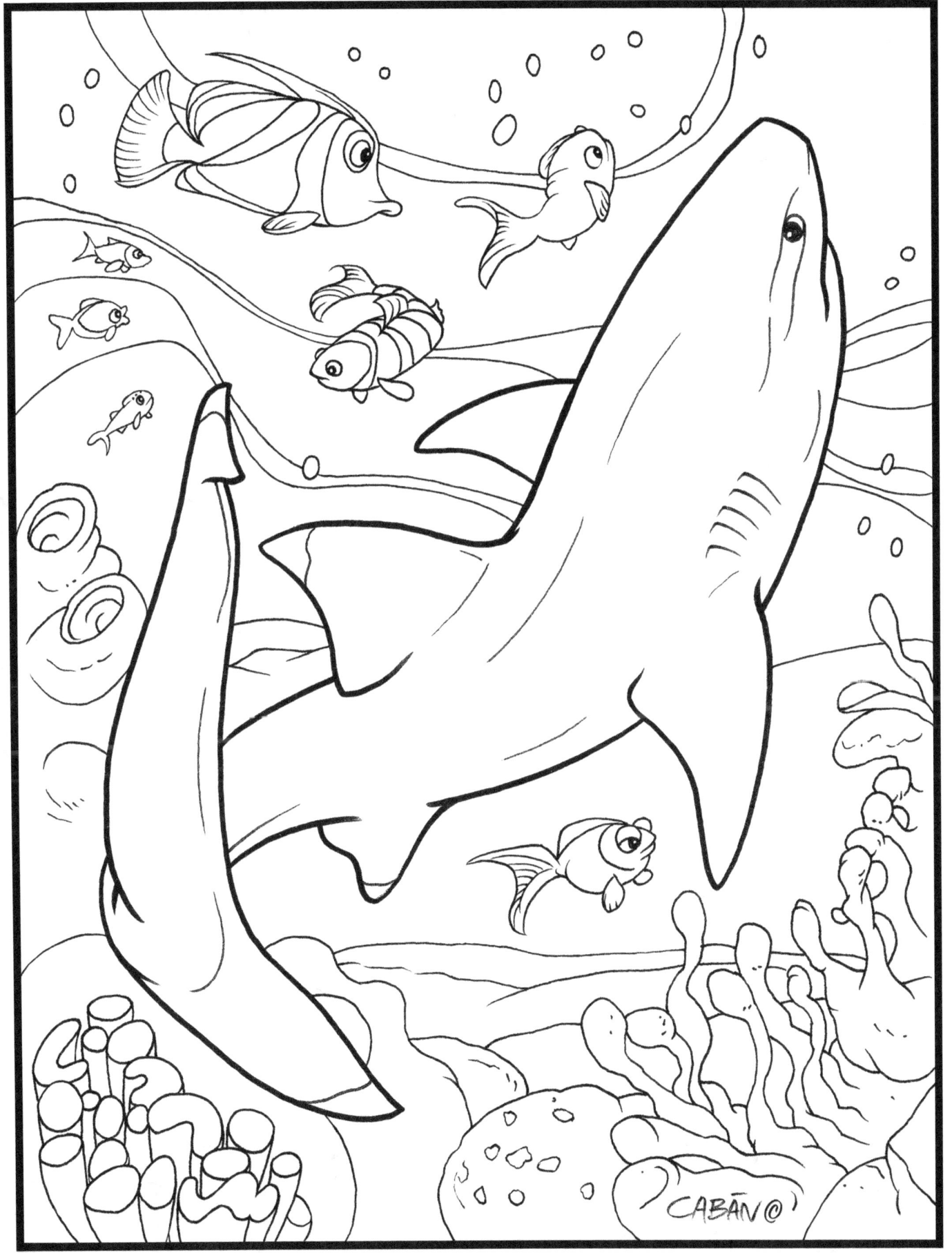

Whitetip Reef Shark

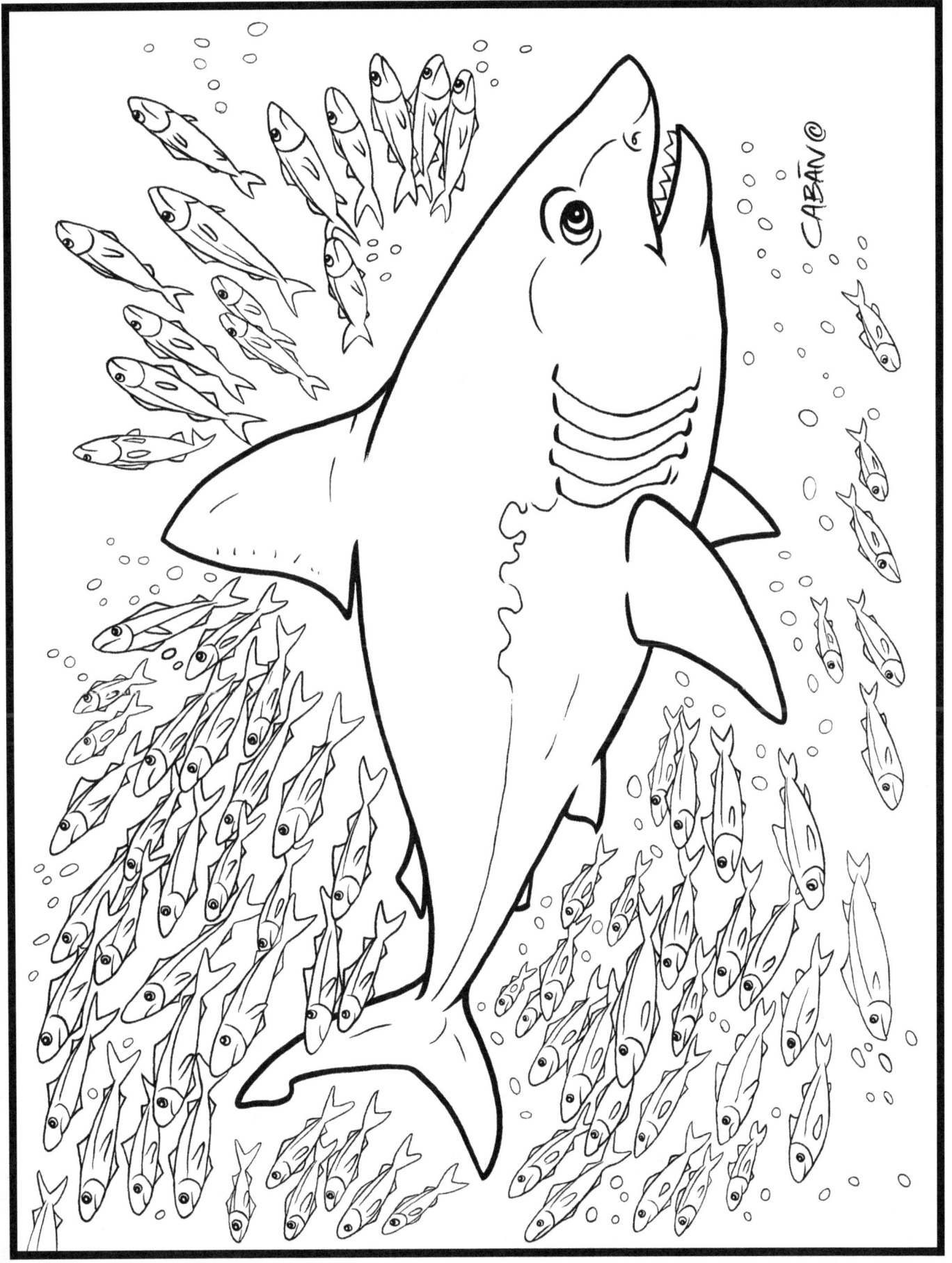

Porbeagle Shark